Small Cosmos

Mary Blackwood

Small Cosmos

Acknowledgements

Many poems in this collection were published, some as earlier versions, in the following newspapers, journals and anthologies: *The Sydney Morning Herald*, 1977; *Tasmanian Review*, 1979; *The Canberra Times*, 1979; *Poetry Australia*, 1983, 1986; *Effects of Light*, 1985; *Angry Women*, 1989; *Island*, 1990, 1993, 2003; *Grimworks*, 1999; *Prospect*, 2014, 2016; *Blue Giraffe*, 2014; *Communion*, 2019.

Thanks are due to those who encouraged and helped me in various ways in the preparation of this collection: Alison Alexander, Christiane Bostock, Karen Knight, Liz McQuilkin, Gina Mercer, Janet Upcher and the late Megan Schaffner.
  Many thanks as well to John, David and Claire Blackwood for their continuing interest and support.

This collection is in memory of my grandmother, Agnes Mary Morris (1895–1983), who between 1971 and 1980 published four poetry books, drawing on poems she had written over many decades.

Small Cosmos
ISBN 978 1 76109 259 6
Copyright © text Mary Blackwood 2022
Cover image: *Squid boats at night, East Coast, Tasmania*,
painting by Mary Blackwood

First published 2022 by
GINNINDERRA PRESS
PO Box 3461 Port Adelaide 5015

Contents

Driving home	7
Utopia	8
Was that the grace of God?	9
The Sisters	10
The Danish physics mistress	11
Can I have a go of the baby?	12
Baby crow at dawn	13
Domestic Blues	14
May I go for a swim, Mother dear?	15
All in good time	16
Grandfather	17
Politician	18
Weekend painter	19
The Catch	20
Old neighbour	21
The green paperweight from Florence	22
Unjust deserts	23
Morning in Saõ Paulo	24
Offering	25
Azalea forest	26
Outer Sister, 1833	27
Cape Barren Island, 1934	28
I am taken to a fish farm in Penang	29
At one moment: 19 August 2014	30
Beijing, June 1989	31
House of cards	32
Elegy	33
After the funeral	34
However	35
Dog	36

Mainstay	37
Mr Neat goes away	38
Topcoat	39
Nightfall	40
The Visit	41
At Your Age	42
Van Canto at the Festival of Voices	43
Before we start	44
Trust me: you know where I am coming from	45
The Interview	46
It is what it is	47
Office Comedian	48
At the Yummy Mummies café	49
A critical praxis	50
Intense and powerfully focused	51
The Known World	52
Jigsaw	53
About the Author	54

Driving home

The houses slip past.
If you press your own pause button
swivel your neck,
you can see for a brief focused second
a family freeze-frame, changing the channel
or closing the venetians, keeping the blue flicker in –
hundreds of slides for the actively curious,
slides, houses, each soul its galaxy.

Slide 12: an adolescent, caught
in aluminium frames, side on to evening.
His truculent cobweb stretches the suburbs.
He has eight teachers, two dogs, and a mother,
three frightened brothers, one desperate headmaster,
partridges, pear trees, a lady from Welfare.
Someone is talking about him at dinner –
unlikely hub to an unremarked universe.

Driving home, you pass thousands of houses.
Each is behind you, each network, in seconds.
Your own small cosmos glows behind your door.
It's cold, and you are late.
     You turn the key.
Across the evening sky come skeins of birds
looping home to welcoming trees.

Utopia

The golden dusty age from six to twelve
my squatting hopscotch childhood
had its fears
of spiders, snakes and sunburn, last one picked
for softball teams, and caught in cloakroom tears
or reading round the Bible class in turn
it might be me who has to say out loud
the verse about the shittim wood of Noah
or Rachel great with child.
Still
I was happy then because I saw
the silver future perfect and I knew
that grown-ups did not blush or weep or bleed.

Was that the grace of God?

Winter Mondays. Catechism.
Hard dark chairs.
Confirmation Day. The scent of flowers.
The altar rail.

We waited reverently
our mouths composed.
So soon the Holy Spirit would be ours.

I knelt in urgent readiness.

The holy words.

Pale hands
were resting on my bristling veil
I strained my soul.

Inert.

The bishop moving
whitely to the next.

The Sisters

Why did they tell us that, the Sisters
their camphor-scented robes
black and swishing,
that nobody would ever buy a nibbled cake
from the bakery, one that had been

licked or bitten or otherwise made disgusting.
And germy.
It would lie unchosen amongst its fellow cakes
each gradually being taken home
and gobbled up.

The lucky ones!

So, girls,
said the Sisters.
Stay pure.

Too young for analogy
not even bleeding
we'd no idea
what the Sisters meant.

The Danish physics mistress

She always wore
    sensible shoes
    a tartan skirt.
We thought she'd had something to do with The War
except that she was so kind.

If you gave the wrong answer she said 'yes very good,
                                        but no.'

Perhaps we took advantage.
She let us roll beads of mercury down our hands
let us bring our knitting to class.

When we heard she'd put her head in the oven
    we wondered if
    it was because of us.

Can I have a go of the baby?

My nephew at four
examines in silence
his unblinking cousin
six weeks in her swaddle.

My nephew asks
for a go of the baby,
turns away soon to a red helicopter.

His mother collects him
and leaving he says
    'instead of this baby
    you should get a dog.'

Baby crow at dawn

I blunder down pale stairs
yellow with resentment
I peel sodden layers
from the furious bundle.
I warm milk.

Fed and dry my daughter scrabbles
in a plastic scatter of toys
    triumphant
finds a dead blowfly
    unashamed
is sick on my foot
    crows with glee.
The house sleeps.
I make porridge.

All over my little city
women are working like this.

It's just gone five.

A fishing boat trails a thin straight line
through the distant silky harbour.

The fisherman starts his work.
He of course will be paid.

Domestic Blues

In the supermarket trolley
I could see a can of peas.
When I swapped them for some lollies
Mother shot me in both knees.

Later in a sea of pumpkin
when my sister threw a plate,
Mother rang the Social Welfare,
had her made a ward of state.

Both of us, impressed by Mother,
went to bed without a bleat
even when we heard her throwing
all the saucepans in the street.

We could hear the sirens wailing
Daddy came in looking pink.
He had spent the weekend sailing
seemed a bit the worse for drink.

'Mother's gone! She thought it better
having set the house on fire
left us just this little letter:
Dinner's in the tumble dryer.'

May I go for a swim, Mother dear?

We are allowed to the edge of the truth.
We lean over carefully, dip toes and fingers.

Over the edge is the rage of the artist
diving through nights with his hands trailing oysters
honing his talents on sharpstones of freedom
clawing his name on the backs of his children.

We are allowed to go paddling, Tuesdays.
We are allowed to the edge of the truth.

All in good time

A clerk since seventeen, at forty-three
his days filed past in tidy groups of weeks,
monotonous.
He kept the ledgers straight,
amended salaries for annual leave
and took his tea behind his desk, alone.

He married once, and clutched a dream.
She left, and he was glad.

Now every evening
he sat with his images
saw the world's loveliness
through a dark prism.

Planning the future
in front of his mirror
he practised expressions
holding his rifle.

Grandfather

In memory of Carl Morris (1888–1971)

What was his wisdom, retired headmaster
in his grey gardening suit, chipping the drive?
We knew he'd had power some time in the past,
a rule over children like us – we were five
and seven, and awed
by his stern kindly photograph
gown, mortar board.

Careful, precise,
he would pen such a nice
curled flowing autograph
in our scruffy, thumbed collections.
He knew Latin inflections
and how to stick stamps in appropriate sections.
But that was not his wisdom. Even then
we had a rough childish sense of his worth.
He'd become all his values, absorbing the Ten
Commandments, breathed daily goodwill upon Earth.

The thought of that wisdom
when time came to die
brought a spiritual tear
to this agnostic eye.

Politician

I slide down the grooves in your hand,
my course is yours.
My quicksilver* progress leaves no mark.
Press me with a finger, I split
into bright little spheres.
You cannot catch me.

When you are tired of trying
I gather myselves.
I am whole again.
Scientists say
there is a slow poison from
knowing me too well.

Quicksilver is the common name for mercury, a heavy silvery metal that is liquid under standard conditions. People who studied chemistry in the 1960s would be familiar with its fascinating properties: a class amusement was to roll it round in a dish and try to pick it up. It is still widely used in manufacturing (for example, in fluorescent lamps and barometers) but its use in clinical instruments like thermometers has greatly reduced because of its toxicity under certain conditions.

Weekend painter

I hold my brush to the sky
the violet underside of clouds
the opalescent sea,
the pale ribbed beach.

Here comes a seascape
ultramarine
sand through the shallows
grey for the driftwood
working perspectives
islands horizons
frowning and measuring
mixing and checking.

The sea curves away in a faultless arc
pelicans glide in the pearly sky
effortless waves
paint themselves perfect.

The Catch

Eighteen
the world spun to your laugh
but you slipped
through the nets of wild boys
to his capturing cove.

There you grew sea-gardens
danced the bright future
you wove his gold children
and sang him through darkness.

Forty
defenceless
you spin to your pain

he is gone   he your harbour
chasing eighteen again.

Bravely into the black water
you go with your broken threads trailing.

Old neighbour

Warm scones
in a gingham twist

pea and ham soup
the week after Christmas

old clever ways
with the old plain things.

Lamb's fry
cottage pie
feed a cold and starve a fever
Friars Balsam
flummery

all those ways
all gone with you.

The green paperweight from Florence

Aunt Hilda never wore the pale blue coat from Paris
in case the sleeves got dirty.
Precious things
lay in the dark of her wardrobe drawers.
She kept out of the sun so her hair colour would last
and tore across the sugar bag so as not to waste a grain.
She gave us packs of floral tissues at Christmas.
Stick thin now –
getting sicker
getting crosser –
she asks me to bring the green paperweight from Florence
the white rug, the blue dish, the lemon plate from Rome
and the little yellow olive bowls
the flower pot, the scissors, the blue-striped blouse
and the Other Cushion –
NOT THIS ONE.
On Christmas Day
here from the nursing home
she gives us each
a stiff embrace
a Christmas card
and a cheque for a thousand dollars.

Unjust deserts

I'm immunised
against premature death.
I jog through the sleeping streets.
I run past the toasty
scent of breakfast.
I'm careful about
my litres of water
my keto diet
my fibre intake.

I work at my standing desk all day
and cycle home.

I lace my shoes
for my evening run.

The future rattles
quietly
inside me
but I cannot hear.

Morning in Saõ Paulo

In doorways men twitch in their sleep
beggars spread cloths on the street
the city hums with heat.

Graffiti web the walls
flies fizz in the garbage
pavements steam.

Just round the corner in their Gucci shoes
young men in black unchain glass doors:
the Aston Martin dealership is open.

At home the cold
bright air is sweet
and everyone is equal
we are told.

Offering

My mother cried so much when we set off
from Cuzco to this high and ancient place.
She must have thought my sandals would be torn
or I would lose my new red winter shawl.

When I come back she'll know how good I've been.
The gods will smile and then the rain will come.

It's very cold up here against the rock.
The men have made a hollow, and they sing.

In 1995, anthropologists discovered the frozen and perfectly preserved body of a young girl who was killed as an offering to the Inca gods on Mount Ampato sometime between 1450 and 1480. It is thought that she came from a noble family in Cuzco, over 250 kilometres away. She has been named Juanita the Ice Maiden, and she rests now in a special museum in Arequipa, in the Andes.

Azalea forest

moss

lichen

      waterfall
   bridge
     iris pond

silence.

All Japan

a poem.

Outer Sister, 1833

You
the one light in
the black of her dying:
eggs from the cormorant,
sea-raven,
fed you.

No one could come to us
wind-savaged granite
under the world
in the heartless dark ocean.

When you are big
I will tell you the story
how – searching for softness –
you mouthed my rough coat.

Outer Sister is a granite and dolerite island, one of about a hundred in the Furneaux Group in Bass Strait, Tasmania. In the 1830s, Henry Maynard lived on the island with his Tasmanian Aboriginal wife Margaret. When she died in childbirth in 1833, claims a local history, the baby was reared on 'lightly coddled cormorant eggs'.

Cape Barren Island, 1934

Anemones fringe salt pools.
Forever the shoreline
sucks and heaves
kelp and shingle
ancient
unsleeping
the stare of the dolerite

landscape and seascape
immune and uncaring.

Women snip calico
women make wreaths.

Cape Barren Island is in the Furneaux Group in Bass Strait. It belongs to the Tasmanian Aboriginal community. In the great polio epidemic of 1934, the island was hard hit, and some died of this terrible disease. The island women made wreaths, and people were laid to rest in shrouds of neatly clipped calico.

I am taken to a fish farm in Penang

The fish farm hand
   lives
on the water
   sits
on two bags of dried fish pellets
   sleeps
in a string hammock.

In the Paragon Plaza
ice clinks on gin.

I wish I hadn't gone.

Milky sea
   heat haze
      doomed fish leaping.

At one moment: 19 August 2014

Exactly as
boats trail white wakes in
the brilliant blue
a child is playing at the creaming shoreline
and green cliffs rise to the endless sky;

exactly then,
across the world
flanked by a black shadow
and bound in orange
a man is kneeling in the desert sand
under the same, the endless sky.

On 19 August 2014, American journalist James Foley was beheaded by Islamic State in Raqqa, Syria.

Beijing, June 1989

Five hundred
five hundred times
with easy barbarism
bullets spray
through their targets
into the wide
community of uncles
sisters
teachers
friends and
Mah jong partners
not to mention
let alone
mothers for whom
the vulnerable back of
a child's head
has made the heart stop
or fathers
who have held small hands
and hold now the bill for the bullet.

the skins of my children
too safe
against my face.

House of cards

In less than ten words
it can all tumble down
the house that you made
with the cards you were dealt:
your happiness house
with the glowing inside.

I'm sorry to say you have cancer...
I'm afraid I don't love you any more...
This is the police: there has been an accident...

From now
the hot stone in your throat.

Elegy

The daily conversation has a core.
Affinities are real. The loving flower
is pure and red no less because it holds
predestined winter in its folded heart.

Yet there is no shield
for pain, no hands
can cradle-child
the shattered self.

In the fluorescent room the knives
were all for me, and mine the healing.

After the funeral

After the funeral
the surge of relief
it's over at last.

On the passenger seat
your order of service
your confident smile.

After the funeral
an embarrassment of casseroles
the black of your absence.

However

However content
with
the empty chair
or
the new wife
with
the absence, the idea of never,
however
adjusted you are
as you move down your paths
and predictable lawns,

still

a rosebush will find you
can still make you bleed
with its stinging reminder
its dart at your finger.

Dog

Dog knew ball.
Dog knew stay.
Dog didn't know goodbye.
Ashes on the shoreline:
dog did not know die.

Mainstay

The roses grew
and the shirts lay down
in their scented folds
and the infant thrived

then
the linchpin
snapped –
she was drowned
she got sick
she returned to work –

so the shirts grew grey
in their rankled piles
and the infant barked
and the roses bit.

Mr Neat goes away

The windows shone
and the white paint gleamed
on the iron lace
and the hedge stood square.

Then
the old man left
with a stroke
or his heart
or to live with Shirl.

So the rust ran brown
down the iron lace
and the weeds looped high
and the old house wept.

Topcoat

Chicken dinner and gooseberry pie
granddaughters come in their party frocks.
Showers and snow mist over the mountain
down the path the chill of winter

how glad he is of his new topcoat!

He writes an outline of his life
for the papers
should anything happen.

Today the weather clears sufficiently
for laundry to dry on the line.
She gets the mail –
a letter from the Superannuation.

She puts his topcoat in the Red Cross bag
and tidies once again the tidy shelves.

Drawing a rug around her as she reads
she aches with loneliness.

Nightfall

In black and white a little boy
stands forlorn on the jetty.
His father waves from the water
at the Box Brownie.

Women simper in sepia
christening dresses trail.
It's all packed away:
tapestries, silver, ninety years' treasures.

The ambulance trolley was first:
down the corridor and into the twilight.
Then, after a fortnight, the removalist, then
the family, with boxes and big plastic bags.

In the nursing home
doors close softly in the corridors.

The Visit

All the people around me are
either demented or dying.
And I'm not.
Extraordinary, isn't it?
I'm happy here though

all the same, I might
up…things…things…up sticks, move to Melbourne
to be with the grandchildren.
When did we last meet, tell me?
Oh yes, of course, of course, where
was that?
I might move to Melbourne although I'm
happy here.
And the extraordinary thing is
that everyone around me is dying or
demented.
And I'm not.

Just think, I'm not demented or dying, although I'm 84.
I am 84, aren't I?
When did we last meet? Oh yes, of course.

Do you have to go? Will you come again and see me?

At Your Age

The physiotherapist tells you
there are three things the matter
with your foot
all of which can be expected
At Your Age:

Achilles tendonitis,
degenerative metatarsal joints and
anterior ankle arthritis.
He mobilises the joint
suggests a range of exercises
is kind to you.

You tell his name
to all your friends
with creaky knees
titanium hips.

They go to him
and when they say
they've been sent by you

he says
Who?

Van Canto at the Festival of Voices

Mad for metal
bobble and stamp
thrust and twist
thump and pound.

Invisible we
in our shapeless coats
rounded and old
feet on the ground.

But our ribs vibrate to the beat
and the singing carries us back
for once we too were sharp and sweet
and we strode the stage in black.

Before we start

A minute's silence
for absent friends
for all of those gone
those who have passed

all of those colleagues
friends and retirees
heads of department
poppies and nannies

all of them gathered
in heaven's bright gardens
all looking down and
sharing a minute.

Trust me: you know where I am coming from

I promise all of you here and now
that I am here for the long haul.

Even though I move
from a comfort zone
on a steep learning curve
at the side of my desk
my playing field will be level
and my goalposts will not move.

I will name up the issues
without fear or favour
and then I will address them
through focus groups   target groups
working parties   taskforces   and
overarching committees.

There is no way known that
I will compare apples with oranges.
I will not rearrange the deckchairs on the
Titanic, neither will I reinvent the wheel.
These are my objectives.

I am humbled by your trust.
Thank you for your time.

The Interview

Weaknesses?
Now that you've asked me, I'd have to say
I'm just too honest, too much integrity for my own good.
That would be my main fault.
After that, I guess it would be
having too high standards.
I'll stay late to complete a job,
I'm a perfectionist when it comes to finishing.
Don't suffer fools gladly either, there's a third fault.

And my strengths?
Well
I'm a people person, love helping others.
If you're struggling with something then I'm there for you
Advising, getting you to see what you should do.
And at the same time
I'm a very strategic, big picture type of person.
I'll knock the big issues into a nutshell for you
and come up with the goods.

When will you be deciding about the job?
Oh.
   Okay.
      I'll wait to hear.

It is what it is

My user-friendly gender-neutral
raft of issues carries me
past rocks of bells and whistles
and the pear-shapes of diversity.
It isn't rocket breaking –
it was bottom-up designed
objectively restructuring
and all grass roots aligned.
When the rubber hits the road
conversations must be had
my raft will push the envelope
to stop me going mad.
I strengthen it with corporate glue
I ramp it up outside the square
I pick it up with open arms –
my raft of issues, always there.

Office Comedian

I'm a bit of a stirrer, bit of a rebel
like a good laugh,
mad sense of humour.
The other day for example, I took down
one of those butch women at the office
you know the sort, can't get a man,
all they need's a good you know, can't say, ladies present.
Told her I'd seen a memo
she was listed for special promotion.

She took us all to lunch
then after she'd paid
I spilt the beans
said I'd misread the name.
She hasn't spoken since, women are like that,
can't take a joke.

I'm in for promotion myself, won't get it of course.
Someone like me rocks the boat.

Too many ideas, people get jealous.
I don't answer to anyone, I'm my own man

bit of a stirrer you see
a bit of a rebel.

At the Yummy Mummies café

I've ordered my lunch
the choice was fantastic

> black quinoa salad with roast broccolini
> hummus and beetroot
> purée of carrot

pickled asparagus
ginger kombucha

> turmeric latte
> and sugarless chocolate

secretly longing
for chops and three veg.

A critical praxis

found poem

Performing spatial labour at the edge
of sensibility and archetype
invisibly perpetuated now
through architecture's discourse and its texts.

I ask how this is knowable, and how
erasure can forensically inquire
into the obfuscation of the past
to lead us where we need to be at last.

Well now.
That is my explanatory note.

My art speaks for itself.

Intense and powerfully focused

found poem

The subtle and restrained
nose offers up lavender
sliced green apple excellent weight
in the mouth while

this second wine has a breathtakingly persistent finish
replete with the hallmark austerity
we've come to expect from the maker
it is almost unbelievably spherical.

The next wine – feminine and delectable
with a charismatic balance
and typical aromas of smoke and apple along
with small red berries – finishes lovely and round

yellow plums   white peaches
and the next one just
kissed with the lightest touch of malolactic
is a demanding wine
a fine balance

pulling dynamically into a linear honed tail
carrying on rich and tight
into the finish.

The Known World

You could know almost everything once
about geometry
philosophy
astronomy
theology –
some people had read every book.

You can know almost everything now
about
contaminants in ice cores
advanced equine dentistry
successive reversal learning
aloe vera: its medical uses
planetary nebulae
or
saliva –
each one its very own book.

You dance on a tiny square
in the infinite grid of knowledge.

Jigsaw

Bits of the giant jigsaw lie on the table.
There's a generous time limit: seventy years.
Eagerly you start.

First the most complicated bits
the jewelled windows in the thatched cottage
children's faces looking out   the courtyard cobblestones.
It's going well.
You've only the background to go
you'll get there easily, with thirty years to spare.
The cottage looks wrong   there's a hole   pieces fall
or change somehow   no convex for the concave.
You start again   almost from the beginning,
more desperate now – time's running on.

Time's up.

You've put something together.
Not what you thought at all
not
much like the picture on the shiny box.

About the Author

Born and educated in Tasmania, Mary Blackwood had a long career in the health industry, first as a clinical psychologist and later in a number of senior management roles, most notably in mental health. She retired in 2013.

Her poems have been published over four decades since the 1970s. Her rhyming children's story *Derek the Dinosaur*, illustrated by Kerry Argent, was first published in 1987 by Omnibus Books, reprinted seven times, and published in America and Korea.

Mary and her family live in Hobart.

www.ingramcontent.com/pod-product-compliance
Lightning Source LLC
Chambersburg PA
CBHW062204100526
44589CB00014B/1946